MONEY
THE ASSEMBLY GUIDE

JACK FALLOWS

Thank you for taking the time to read my book.

My aim is for you to feel confident that your money is organised in a way that provides you with security and the freedom to concentrate on enjoying your life.

By the end of this book, I hope you achieve that 'tidy house / tidy mind' feeling ... about your finances.

Best wishes,

Jack.

This book is dedicated to my beautifully brilliant nieces and nephew:

Jazzy, Izzy, Willy, Evie and Lottie.

I am immensely proud of you and cannot wait to see you flourish in life.

Love, Uncle Jack.

Foreword

Finances are not my strong point. My ignorance keeps me in bliss, a bit like the head-burying ostrich analogy Jack uses. However, that is not a very productive or adult way of going through life. Reading this book has helped open my eyes to my financial situation and to take important steps to improve my financial fitness.

I admire Jack's intelligent application of Maslow's hierarchy of needs to create his own tower, the Fallows' Financial Hierarchy of Needs. By working through the chapters, assisted by Jack's useful and entertaining building-block metaphor, I have been able to see clearly what I need to do to be more organised with my money. Jack's writing style makes for an enjoyable read on a serious subject. He simplifies the key elements of his theory into understandable bite-size chunks, so I was able to absorb and apply the information with ease.

I would highly recommend that everyone, whether you think you have your finances in order or not, check out Jack's financial hierarchy of needs and where you stand in relation to his theory. After which, you can use this book as a guide to help you achieve and assemble your finances in a way that is resilient and rewarding.

The least anyone deserves, regarding their finances, is someone who will thoughtfully explain their money in a way that is easily understood and, dare I say it, entertaining. Jack does exactly that.

After reading Jack's book I truly understand what it is to have that 'tidy house, tidy mind' feeling about your finances.

Steve Judge
Multi-award winning global speaker, coach, author and two-times paratriathlon World Champion

Acknowledgements

I would like to thank the following magnificent people for their invaluable input. I greatly appreciate your time, support and inspiration.

Georgia Chadderton	Suraya Khan
Rob Chadderton	Dave Leddington
Richard Charles	Paul Naylor
Sophie Clarke	Hannah Nolloth
Nick Godfrey	Matthew O'Loughlin
Pete Griffiths	Jamie Porter
Duncan Howie	Guy Robinson
Sarah Howie	Jane Simmonds
Steve Judge	Alex Stone

Contents

About the author

Jack Fallows, a financial adviser based in Shrewsbury, Shropshire, is popular for his use of unique and memorable metaphors whilst explaining complex topics, as you will witness throughout this book.

He provides advice to business owners, people who want to retire before the ever-increasing state pension age and folk who have other things they would much rather focus on, so appreciate a plan being developed for their finances to keep them on track throughout life.

A little about Jack's background – upon deciding that university sounded like an expensive way of maintaining a multi-year state of inebriation whilst racking-up high levels of debt, Jack resolved to go travelling around the world, to experience different cultures and the values they live by.

Many months and a gallon of factor-50 suncream later (Jack is a redhead), Jack had explored countries such as Cambodia, Vietnam, Thailand, Fiji, Australia and New Zealand, to name a few. At this point, Jack felt ready to commit to the world of work, but in his way.

Jack wanted a degree in business, but remained adamant there was a less costly, and more effective, way than going to university. So, he swapped the suncream for engine oil and started at the bottom of the ladder in the manufacturing and engineering industry. Before long, Jack progressed to positions of management and put forward a proposal to his employer that he felt provided a more financially savvy way of getting that business degree he coveted – he asked his employer to sponsor him. Thus, Jack proceeded on an arduous journey of studying during his evenings and weekends.

It was hard work but, by the end, Jack had his business degree, zero debt, and had simultaneously purchased and sold not only his first property, but his second too. The financial bug had bitten him.

However, upon being bitten by that bug, a side effect that Jack didn't anticipate was the feeling of being on a conveyor belt – one that demands that you to continue working to pay the bills. Yes, this is life for the majority of people, yet there is a huge difference in happiness and sense of purpose between who that do a job they love, and those who do a job for no reason other than to pay the bills. Hence the phrase, living to work.

This didn't sit right with Jack. He wanted to do something that truly helped others; he yearned to shine a light on an area where others have little knowledge; he aspired to run his own business; he longed to create and maintain a culture that helps others achieve that 'tidy house, tidy mind' feeling you get when you've completed chores, but with a topic that is pertinent to us all.

Financial advice ticked all those boxes.

Whilst working in manufacturing and engineering, Jack didn't understand what a pension was; he didn't know how income tax worked; he couldn't fathom his payslips. Like most of us, Jack had to figure out everything as he went – needless to say, his first mortgage was an eye-opener! So, Jack knows what it feels like to have left the education system with a precise knowledge of algebra, but not so much as a basic understanding of how to manage your money in a way that is safe and sustainable.

Now Jack creates financial plans for his clients, the outcome of which is much more than the sum of the numbers they contain. Jack's plans provide his clients with a sense of security, a feeling of confidence and the freedom for his clients to focus on the things they enjoy most in life, without niggling money worries.

As you will discover in the following pages, *Money: The Assembly Guide* is the next step in Jack's mission – to spread his knowledge far beyond his client base and to provide people of all ages and backgrounds with the tools necessary to structure their money in a way that provides them with security, confidence and freedom.

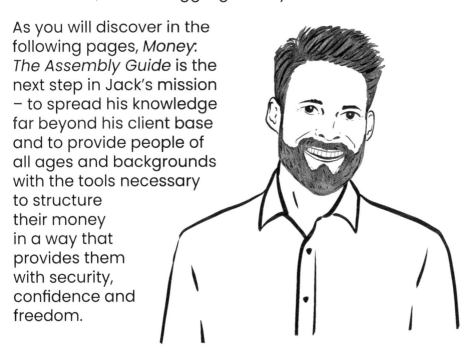

Feel free to contact me...

If you're reading this book, it is highly likely there is something you would like to improve upon regarding your money. The reason I help people with their money is because I want to give them the same 'tidy house / tidy mind' feeling I get when I know my finances are fit and healthy.

My mission isn't to amass as much money as humanly possible because that doesn't necessarily correlate with happiness. Instead, having a sense of security about my money gives me the confidence to do other things that I enjoy doing with my time, like spending time with family, friends and doing hobbies. *That*, for me, directly correlates with my happiness.

So, if you would like a hand getting that 'tidy house / tidy mind' feeling about your finances, please feel free to contact me and I will be happy to help.

By scanning this QR code, you can:

- send me an email
- come along to my next event
- join my informative monthly newsletter, *The Reality Cheque*
- connect with me on LinkedIn
- follow me on Facebook.

Introduction

I know what it's like to feel overwhelmed by money because, believe it or not, I wasn't born a financial adviser. Until I began working in finance, I was much like you – learning as I went along. But finance isn't really the area of your life where you want to learn from your mistakes, as they can be costly.

I also understand that thinking about money, at its worst, can be worrying and, at its best, can be boring. There are plenty of things you would much rather spend your time doing. However, those things usually require money in one way or another.

Herein lies the purpose of this book. *Money: The Assembly Guide* will show you how to structure your money in such a way that it is strong enough to weather everything life has to throw at it, all in an easily understandable and light-hearted way.

Have you ever felt that 'tidy house, tidy mind' feeling when you have finally mustered the motivation to complete the household tasks adulting requires of you?

Afterwards, you can relax and enjoy life in a way that feels even sweeter, right? You can concentrate on doing things that genuinely make you happy, without worrying.

This is the feeling that *Money: The Assembly Guide* will give you.

Learning as we go

We aren't really taught about money at school. We're given a basic understanding of notes and coins, and that's about it.

Exam papers in primary and secondary school ask us to answer questions such as 'If Priscilla has £5 and bananas are 50p each, how many bananas can Priscilla purchase?' Other than that, our financial education is left entirely to us. We learn as we go.

More to the point, if you were anything like me at school, you were left daydreaming about what kind of parent would inflict such a name on their child, rather than the cost of fictional bananas.

Further still, today's children would ponder why Priscilla isn't using a contactless card!

Is society spending your money for you?

Alongside our lack of financial education, we also live in a society where our accomplishments are measured largely by the material objects we own.

I'm sure you've looked at someone – a friend, colleague or even a family member – and thought, 'they're doing well'.

You may have thought, 'they must be making and saving lots of money to go on nice holidays, park two posh cars on the drive, and purchase the latest gadgets like air pods or the newest air-blowing contraption from Dyson'.

But do you ever stop and think how they are purchasing all these things? Do you ever consider that they might be buying it all on a credit card? Or if they have taken out loans? Do you ever think they might not be saving at all, and are living perilously close to the breadline, should they lose their source of income?

Sure, they may have enough disposable income to do and purchase all those fancy things. However, it's dangerous to try and replicate their way of living for three reasons:

1. You might be jumping without realising into the same scary position they are in, where it could all come tumbling down very quickly.
2. You might be trying to replicate a standard of living that you cannot afford.
3. You might be killing yourself to achieve this materialistic lifestyle when you don't actually want it, you just think you do (more about this later).

The epiphany that inspired this book

When I am asked what I do for a living, the response, after stating I am a financial adviser, is almost always along the lines of:

'Oh really? Can you help me to do X?' 'X' can be any of the following:

- Sort out my pensions so I can retire before my state pension age?
- Grow my money in a way that's better than the shoddy interest rates offered by banks at the moment?

- Pay for some form of expenditure in the future, like home refurbishment, a bucket-list holiday or a little property by the sea?

Whilst I appreciate the questions above reflect things that are important to the people who ask them, I believe our lack of education around money at school means our priorities are in the wrong order.

In other words, each of those statements is fundamentally flawed.

The statements above assume that nothing will go wrong in the meantime – that you won't have any financial hardship or ill health, and that the people dependent upon you won't either.

However, our finances and health rarely remain consistent throughout our lives.

Further still, our finances and health aren't even reliant entirely upon *us*.

They can worsen due to forces outside of our control – redundancy, recession, illnesses, or accidents ... the list goes on.

The neighbour who started it all

It was during a fleeting conversation with a neighbour,

who had just asked what I do for a living, that the idea for this book struck me. The neighbour, upon learning what my profession was, unhesitatingly embarked upon peppering me with a series of questions. Where were the best places to invest their money? How could they fund their children through private education? How to retire early? Should they rent out their property when they eventually move? I know – I was only taking the bins out!

However, there was one thing the questions all had In common: they assumed the future would be kind to them, regardless of the decision they made.

Meet Maslow

In 1943, Abraham Maslow, an American psychologist who shares an amusing resemblance to Manuel from *Fawlty Towers*, published a paper called '*A Theory of Human Motivation*'. In it, he proposed that people have five sets of basic human needs.

In short, the theory suggests that as each need is fulfilled, the desire to achieve the next should start.

PSYCHOLOGIST, ABRAHAM MASLOW (NOT MANUEL FROM FAWLTY TOWERS)

Thus, at any given point, the need we are yet to fulfil *should* 'monopolise our consciousness' (lovely phrasing, Maslow) or, in plain English, be our main focus until it is achieved.

What's the point in Maslow's theory? Well, it's a way of constructing a safe, healthy and satisfying lifestyle.

Over time, Maslow's list of needs has come to be known as a 'hierarchy of needs'. The hierarchy is often represented as a pyramid, looking somewhat like the one below; however, I have adapted it slightly to include an element that, according to my teenage nieces and nephew, is absolutely fundamental to a human's existence – WiFi.

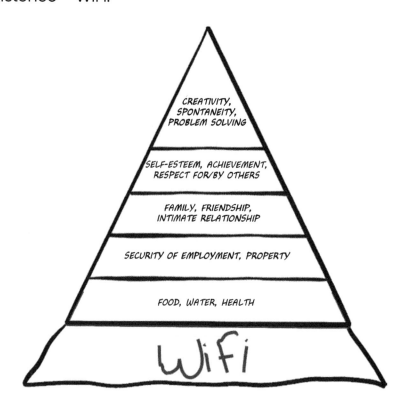

Maslow himself proposed a couple of weaknesses in his hierarchy of needs:

1. The impact society has on someone's perception of their needs.

2. What a person desires is not always the most essential for their current wellbeing.

Therefore, it is easy to see why, when someone finds out I'm a financial adviser, the first thing they want to know about is the 'fun stuff' – retiring early, the best investments, renting out a property, etc. – instead of ensuring they are financially secure.

This is because we haven't been educated about our finances properly in the first place. Again, there is a huge amount of pressure on us from society to buy a better car, home, or Dyson air-blowing thingy instead.

In essence, we haven't been taught how to prioritise our finances to ensure we are secure in the short-term and have financial freedom in the long-term; we haven't been given the architectural blueprint; we've skipped The Assembly Guide.

In the same way as you may purchase a swanky piece of Swedish furniture from IKEA and, after a few meatballs, unnecessary tea candles and a monotonous drive home, decide to ditch the assembly guide that will hold your hand through the construction process – you can work it out for yourself. A period of time later (inevitably the estimated minutes quoted on the assembly guide x1.5), you stand back from your newly erected piece of furniture, full of pride at your fantastic feat of engineering. That is, until you spot a lonesome bolt lingering on the carpet; your furniture isn't quite as rigid as it was in the showroom.

When constructing financial plans for the future, people often make a similar mistake.

Time for a new hierarchy?

Therefore, in this book, I invite you to take a step back and look at your *financial* hierarchy of needs. We're not looking at other people's pyramids or considering what society thinks *our* pyramid should look like. Instead, we're looking at making sure *our* pyramid is strong enough to survive all weathers.

Below is my adapted version of Maslow's pyramid, which I have coined The Fallows' Financial Hierarchy of Needs. This, I invite you to climb.

1) Insurance

If anything is going to stand upright, it needs to be built on solid foundations. Every plan you have about your future is built upon the assumption that you will be healthy enough

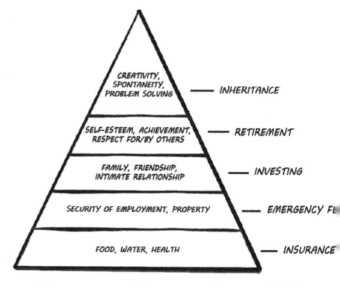

to earn an income all the way until you get there. This is why I recommend the foundation for anyone's financial plan is to protect their chief asset – health.

2) Emergency fund

As Forrest Gump famously proclaimed, 's**t happens'. So, you need a fund to deal with it. You may be great at saving, but unless you have a pot to call upon when, for example, your boiler or car breaks down, you will end up spending those hard-earned savings on the emergency.

Maslow suggests, 'anything that has the potential to thwart your basic human needs should be considered a psychological threat'. Maslow suggests, 'anything that has the potential to thwart your basic human needs should be considered a psychological threat'. Now, this is slightly strong wording – however, in 1943, the guy was in the middle of a world war, so we'll let him off. But he does have a good point. Ignoring the initial stages of the pyramid should be considered a threat to the standard of living you enjoy (for example, neglecting to use that lonely IKEA bolt on the floor).

3) Investing
Often, our thoughts about the future include enjoying it with others or, as Maslow puts it, 'hunger for affectionate relationships with people'. When we think of saving for a holiday, a new kitchen, or a bucket-list experience like scuba diving, it is rare that we think about doing these things by ourselves. We usually envisage sharing these memories with other people. Constantly putting experiences on a credit card, or continuously taking out loans is a recipe for ensuring that you will not be able to maintain them in the future. That's why investing is important at this point, so that you can continue doing the things that are important to you.

4) Retirement
Maslow suggests that the next rung of the pyramidal ladder, relating to esteem, can be described as 'independence and freedom'. This is what my clients

express when they talk about retirement – the independence and freedom to, fundamentally, do more things they like, and fewer things they don't like. They want to enjoy life whilst no longer working, which requires a sense of security.

As well as independence and freedom, Maslow said that the feeling of being 'useful and necessary in the world' also has a lot to do with happiness and maintaining good mental health. I'm not a doctor, but having something to live for, and being able to do it, feels like a good way to live longer and to enjoy retirement to the fullest.

5) Inheritance

Future generations and inheritance – these are things my clients often worry about. I understand. Having someone you love benefit from your hard work is a satisfying thought, but it makes no sense to think about it until you have secured your other, more rudimentary, needs further down the hierarchy, as the money may be needed before you reach that point.

Moreover, there is no point in thinking about what you are going to pass on to others if you haven't saved or preserved it in the first place. After all, you can't give something away that you don't own! So, if you've spent all your savings during retirement, or sold your house to pay for a care home, it's futile thinking about how you can give those assets away, as you no longer own them.

To be satisfied is the exception, not the rule.

In 1943, Maslow suggested, 'in our society, satisfied people are the exception'.

It feels like things haven't changed that much in the past 80 years, as we live in a world where we constantly compare ourselves to other people's display of (contrived) perfection on social media.

But it doesn't have to be this way!

You can be the exception to Maslow's rule.

This is what this book is going to help you with.

This book will show you exactly how to reprioritise the way you think about your money and, as a result, feel good about it.

That way, you can simultaneously gain a greater sense of financial security *and* financial freedom. That's a win-win, wouldn't you agree?

The good news

To get the most out of this book you do not already need to know:

- How to invest your money
- All things pensions, and whether they are geared toward your version of retirement
- Whether your estate is exposed to inheritance tax.

Why? Not because I'm a financial adviser gone rogue.

But because you can't possibly think about these things constructively until you have secured the rungs of the pyramid that structurally support them.

In the following chapters, we will strip back your relationship with money, recalibrate your financial priorities and reset them to be strong, healthy and sustainable.

Time to ditch the pyramid

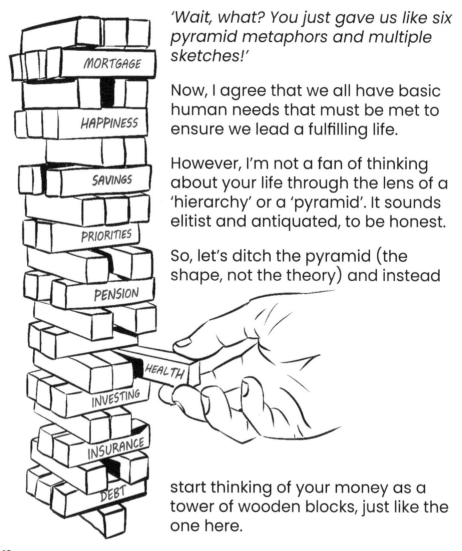

'Wait, what? You just gave us like six pyramid metaphors and multiple sketches!'

Now, I agree that we all have basic human needs that must be met to ensure we lead a fulfilling life.

However, I'm not a fan of thinking about your life through the lens of a 'hierarchy' or a 'pyramid'. It sounds elitist and antiquated, to be honest.

So, let's ditch the pyramid (the shape, not the theory) and instead start thinking of your money as a tower of wooden blocks, just like the one here.

Your lifestyle, funded by your finances, is much like the tower to the left. Its ability to stand up over time is directly related to its stability. If it is on shoddy foundations, it will come tumbling down with the slightest movement.

The lower down the weaknesses are in this structure, the more unstable it will be.

That is why I suggest you prioritise your finances in the order previously described. Here's the list, to jog your memory ...

1. Insurance

2. Emergency fund

3. Investing

4. Retirement

5. Legacy.

This approach to your finances will prevent you from copying your friends, colleagues or family, or folding to the pressures of society. With this approach, you will build your pyra-, I mean tower, on concrete foundations.

Chapter summaries

I'll add a set of key points to remember at the end of each chapter for two reasons:

1. We cover lots of information in each chapter, so I want to make it as easy as possible for you to absorb.
2. This (hopefully) isn't a 'burn after reading' book. It's here to help you reprioritise your relationship with money, which can't be done overnight. So, I want to make it easy for you to revisit and find what you need.

Key points to remember

- Our main issue when it comes to finances is prioritising unwisely.
- We often don't realise that to be successful financially, we need strong foundations.
- According to Abraham Maslow, there are five basic needs for every human. This theory is often presented in a pyramid structure, and the level you're on should be your focus until you have fulfilled it. You can then move on to the level above.
- Whilst in theory this is good, Maslow also acknowledged there were flaws: pressure from society and what you desire aren't necessarily what's best for you.
- Think of finances as a wooden tower to highlight the importance of a stable structure, built upon solid foundations.
- Finally, I suggest you prioritise your finances in the following order: Insurance > Emergency Fund > Investing > Retirement > Legacy.
- This book is The Assembly Guide to building your *financial* hierarchy of needs.

1 What's your Plan A?

What does your future look like?

As I mentioned in the introduction, the purpose of this book is to help you prioritise your finances so that you always make plans for the future built upon solid foundations.

Why would you want to do that? To give you the greatest chance of making your ideal future a reality. I refer to your ideal future as your 'Plan A'; anything else is a compromise.

But before we look at your priorities, it's important to understand what you want your Plan A to look like.

Not sure what you want to achieve in the future? I'd like to reassure you that, when I meet a new client, it's very rare that they have a firm grasp of what they want to achieve.

And for those who do know, they often don't know *why* they want to achieve it.

Not letting the tail wag the dog

If you assess your finances and then adjust your lifestyle to suit, it's like letting the tail wag the dog. By letting your finances control your goals, you are allowing yourself to be at the mercy of your money. And no one wants that. Instead, think about what you want your future to look like first (your Plan A).

It's important to note that your finances *will* control what you are able to achieve to a large extent. Therefore, I'm not suggesting you make a wish list of all the things you want, and financial advice will magically make them appear. Again, this is about prioritising. If you are aware of the things that are most important to you now, you will prioritise them accordingly and will be less likely to take decisions that jeopardise them.

Two questions to predict your future

How do you understand what you want your future to look like?

I ask two questions in every meeting. They are simple but can be hard to answer. They are:

1. What are the most important things to you in life?
2. What does money mean to you?

Let's break them down.

1) What are the most important things to you in life?

People's immediate response to this question is usually financial and goes along the lines of 'to make sure I am/ we are comfortable financially'.

But is this *really* the most important thing to you in the world? So, when I get the above response, I like to delve a little deeper to get to the real answer.

When I do this, the answers I get are more like the following, in no particular order:

● Health, both physical and mental

1 WHAT'S YOUR PLAN A?

- Good relationship with family
- Time to do hobbies
- Spending time with friends
- Being a great parent
- Taking care of my parents in their old age.

These answers are extremely important. They are the 'north star' for your Plan A, giving you something meaningful to guide you in the right direction.

Whether consciously or subconsciously, the greater the extent to which you fulfil these priorities, the happier you are likely to be. Therefore, your finances should be constructed to help ensure you can attain them.

Then, the next question ...

2) What does money mean to you?

Now, you might be thinking, 'erm, well it means I can buy things, stupid!' Fair enough, you're right.

However, the intention of this question isn't to check your understanding of money in a transactional sense. It's intended to help you understand your relationship with money. It's this relationship that forms all your habits when thinking about, and using, money.

Here are some real-life responses I have received in answer to this question:

- Security – 'My family didn't have much money growing up. So, now I have money, I'm scared I'll lose it. Therefore, to me, it means not having to live like I did growing up and preventing my children having the same upbringing I did, where we had a cold house and next to no Christmas presents'

● Family – 'It's the way I make sure my family is the happiest it can be. It pays for a roof over our heads, food on the table, clothes on the kids' backs and holidays'

● Freedom – 'I don't know exactly what I want to do or where I want to go in the future, as we evolve over time. However, I do know that I don't want money to restrain me from leading a healthy and happy life when I get there'

Again, the answers to the questions above are the North Star to guide you towards your Plan A.

Next up, brutal honesty!

The next step involves you being very honest with yourself when it comes to your money habits.

If you aren't, you will constantly lull yourself into a false sense of security or, worse still, you'll forever be at the mercy of your finances – picture a gigantic dog's tail wagging you all over the place!

One way you can do this is by understanding your habits when you think about and use money. To make things easier, here are some more sketches...

FOUR MONEY PERSONALITIES

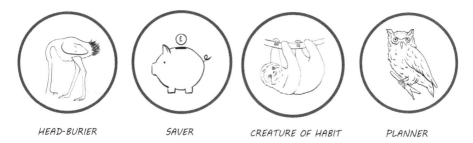

HEAD-BURIER   SAVER   CREATURE OF HABIT   PLANNER

1) Head-burier

These people are waiting for luck to bless them with money, maybe by winning the lottery. They find money a scary topic and, as a result, have plunged their head into the sand where they can ignore their bills, payslips, advice from friends and parents and the news. The great thing about this habit is that the people with it can proceed through life in a state of bliss, as nothing appears to threaten the standard of living they enjoy. The downside is that, when life eventually throws an inevitable curve ball, they will not see it until it is too late and their resilience to challenges is weak.

2) Saver

These admirable fellows work hard and save hard in equal measures. They have developed the brilliant habit of putting some of their money away each month, and they will not spend money unless they own it. This enables them to build up great resilience to life's challenges, and they will not be forced to do things that put them in difficult positions, such as using credit cards. However, these people often tend to get carried away, taking frugality to a whole new level – they never spend their money! Whilst it might sound lovely to have plenty of cash around you, it doesn't sound quite as attractive to think you could live a life working hard, saving hard and playing poorly.

3) Creature of habit

These souls need a bit of encouragement. They delay doing the things they know they need to, not because they are scared, but because they find it ever so boring. They would much rather spend their time focussing on the things in life that make them happy. The upside of this is that they lead very fulfilling lives, doing lots of things that put a smile on their face, like holidaying, buying nice clothes and spending time with friends and family.

However, the downside of this behaviour is that the very thing the cherish the most – their lifestyle – is exactly what will suffer if they are faced with financial challenges, as they haven't put any of the safeguards in place to withstand anything other than the good times.

4) Planner

These wise beings are strategic. They develop plans for their finances and commit to them. This is a terrific behaviour, as it means they strive to do the right things to protect both their money and what is most important to them in life. Yet, whilst their actions are well-intended, they can suffer from ALBOK syndrome (a little bit of knowledge). In my experience, this can unintentionally put them in some perilous positions that, ironically, they would not have ended up in if it were not for trying to perform some financial DIY. We've all been there – just remember the IKEA example.

As you can see from the four money personality types above, there are a range of habits that you can adopt when thinking about, and using, your money. Each has positive and negative elements. Therefore, it is important that you acknowledge your current relationship with money, to know the useful traits you need to hold on to, and the areas you would benefit from improving upon.

A good outcome from this chapter is that it has set you on course to start building your Plan A. Moreover, this should motivate you to focus on ensuring your finances are aligned to your priorities, as opposed to the pressure society puts upon you.

So, here are those two exceedingly simple, but exceptionally hard-to-answer questions again. See if you can answer them, and begin understanding your Plan A ...

1. What are the most important things to you in life?
2. What does money mean to you?

Key points to remember

● Most people don't know what they want their future to look like – their Plan A.
● Those who do probably don't know the reason why they want those things.
● To get to the bottom of what you want out of your future and why, you need to ask yourself two very important questions:
  1) What are the most important things to you in life?
  2) What does money mean to you?

- The answers to these questions are the North Star for your Plan A – your motivation for aligning your finances with that which is most important to you.
- Once you've answered these questions, it's time to be honest with yourself and understand your money habits.
- Now you understand what you want your Plan A to look like, it's time to protect it …

2 Insurance

What's your most valuable asset?

I realise insurance isn't the most exciting topic in the world.

However, insurance is the first and most important step in building the foundations for a solid financial plan. In short, if you do not insure your most valuable asset, you could end up spending your hard-earned savings and investments on something undesirable.

But what is your most valuable asset? (It's probably not what you think it is.)

How we look at safety

Now, we've all thought about where we want to be, and what we want to be doing, at a particular point in the future. However, when we do this, we make the assumption that we will have good health all the way until we get there; we assume our journey will not be derailed at any point.

INSURANCE

WHAT'S YOUR
MOST VALUABLE ASSET?

EVERYTHING
ELSE

YOUR
HEALTH

It sucks, but life is rarely that kind.

This is why insurance needs to be the first item on the list for anyone looking to make sure their finances are as healthy as possible.

Insurance is the concrete foundation upon which all your plans sit – it's the base of your financial tower.

Introducing Mark and Lisa

Mark and Lisa are fictional characters based on a wide range of clients I have worked with. So, if you are called Mark or Lisa and are reading this, don't panic (or ask for a percentage of the book sales!).

I have included Mark and Lisa to help explain my points with real-life examples.

Some things you need to know about Mark and Lisa:

- Both are age 49
- Mark is an architect (sole owner of his Limited Company)
- Lisa is a Human Resources manager (employed)
- They have three daughters (ages 29, 27 and 23) – two have left home, one is still living at home
- They have two grandchildren, with more on the horizon.

What you need to know about Mark and Lisa's priorities:

- They don't like the thought of retiring at their state pension age (67) – instead, they want to retire at 60

- During retirement they don't want to live like church mice – they still want a couple of holidays per year, a new car every three or so years each, to see their children regularly and look after their grandchildren
- They want to repay the mortgage on their home and their rental property by age 60; they would then like to sell the rental property and use the money to buy a little holiday home by the sea in Wales
- They want to contribute to their daughters' home deposits (two out of three daughters left to go) and help with the cost of their weddings (three to go).

They aren't asking for the earth, are they?

So, I asked Mark and Lisa, 'what are your most valuable assets?'

They replied with the following:

1) Their home
2) Their rental property
3) Their cars.

Stress-testing Mark and Lisa's priorities

OK. Considering we have just established Mark and Lisa's most valuable assets, let's explore a couple of scenarios that could conceivably happen to them.

Example scenario 1

Mark has a car accident. Luckily, he survives. However, he suffers a serious concussion and a broken wrist.

This means he is unable to work at all for three weeks whilst his concussion heals. He is also unable to work properly for a further three weeks, as he has a cast on his wrist, which prevents him from using his computer or driving.

As Mark runs his own business, he doesn't get sick pay.

Example scenario 2

Lisa is diagnosed with breast cancer. Luckily, the cancer is operable, but she requires chemotherapy. In total, she spends 18 months off work. Lisa is entitled to good sick pay – three months at 100% pay, then another three months at 50% pay. After that, she has Statutory Sick Pay (around £99.35 per week) for 28 weeks (figures correct as of 2023).

What are the consequences for Mark and Lisa?
- Their savings would have to be used for Mark's time off work, to pay for his share of the bills
- Mark could pay for someone to fill his directing role in his business
- Lisa would have to dip into their savings to cover the period where she is moved to Statutory Sick Pay.

What are the knock-on effects?
- Less money for holidays
- Dipping into the funds saved for their daughters' first home deposits and weddings
- Reduced funds for retirement.

Plus, don't forget the pressure this puts on the family:

- Stress
- Worry
- Arguments between Mark and Lisa due to pressure.

Could these scenarios conceivably happen to you?

Now, Mark and Lisa aren't naïve, they know that insurance is important. For example, they have building insurance for their house, as it is a mandatory requirement from their mortgage company to have it in place. However, they also choose to have contents insurance, which is not mandatory for the mortgage.

The rationale behind their decision was to ensure that if, for example, their bathroom flooded, they would be able to replace the furniture, carpets, light fittings, TV, etc. in the living room below the bathroom, as well as the damage done to the bathroom and building in general.

They also insure their cars. They could have Third Party Fire and Theft insurance, but both choose to have fully comprehensive, as they want to protect their cars against accidental damage. They are very expensive assets after all.

Nevertheless, Mark and Lisa made the common mistake of misidentifying their most valuable assets when putting in place insurance policies.

They put their properties and cars above their health.

Let me illustrate this for you:

- Their house is worth £330,000
- Their rental property is worth £220,000

• Their cars are £51,000 and £31,500 respectively.

Therefore, in total, the assets they believe are most valuable are worth £632,500.

That is, of course, a significant sum. However, they do not own 100% of their properties and cars.

After deducting their mortgages and the part of the cars they are financing, they actually own £550,000 worth of assets.

Mark and Lisa each earn £55,000 per year before tax.

Therefore, their combined income within five years would equal the value of their 'most valuable assets'.

Ah, so their income is their most valuable asset, right? Wrong!

Claiming your income is your most valuable asset yet again makes another assumption that you are healthy enough to earn it.

This means your most valuable asset is actually your health, *then* your income.

Common reasons people choose not to have health insurance

So, what stops people insuring their most valuable asset, besides misidentifying it?

Here are some common reasons:

1. 'It's too expensive.'
2. 'I don't need it, my business (Limited Company) will keep paying me.'
3. 'I don't need it, I have sick pay via my employer.'
4. 'I will sort it out, but at a later date, as I've got good health at the moment.'
5. 'I don't know enough about it.'
6. 'I'm too busy right now.'

In Mark and Lisa's case, they found excuses two and three most convenient respectively.

However, as we have seen through stress-testing the example scenarios above (which have *actually* happened to people I have met in the past), these excuses wouldn't provide enough cover to prevent Mark and Lisa's Plan A from being derailed.

For those who have chosen to take out health insurance, you're not off the hook yet.

I meet people who, in advance, *have* realised the importance of their health in making sure their Plan A stays on track *and* have chosen to do something about it.

Unfortunately, this category of people often ends up implementing insurance policies that do not provide comprehensive cover against the things life is most likely to throw at them.

Three types of health insurance and their hidden weaknesses[1]

1) Life Assurance

Life Assurance is usually put in place when you buy a house, so the mortgage can be repaid by the people inheriting it, which is usually your partner or family.

The problem is though, depending on your age, you are over ten times more likely to take time off work due to illness or accident than to die before you reach your state pension age. Therefore, during your working life, Life Assurance only covers you for the least likely event that could happen regarding your health. It also doesn't protect you from spending your savings if you have to take time off work. And, depending on your level of cantankerousness (yes, that is a word, I checked), you might be inclined to think that, if you're dead, receiving a sum of money to repay your debts is the least of your worries.

2) Critical Illness Insurance

This pays a lump sum if you are diagnosed with an illness covered by the policy. So the likelihood of it paying out depends on the comprehensiveness of the policy.

---

1 For clarity, when I use the term 'health insurance' I'm not referring to 'private medical care', which is provided in a private hospital. Instead, I am referring to insurance policies that provide the owner with money in various forms in the event of their ill health or accident or provide a sum to their intended recipients in the event of their death.

However, some cheaper policies cover so few illnesses that that they might as well be called 'Life Assurance', as they are only likely to pay out if you pass away! So, it is wise to check the comprehensiveness of your policy.

I'm sorry – the mood does get lighter shortly, but we do need to acknowledge the importance of insurance first.

3) Income Protection

If you are unable to perform your occupation, as diagnosed by a medical professional (not yourself, due to a hangover) your income can be replaced by an insurance company via a policy called Income Protection. The time that elapses before the insurance company pays you, how long the pay

you for and how much they pay you is decided by you (within limits, of course). So, this type of insurance fills in a lot of the gaps left by critical illness insurance, as that insurance only pays after you are diagnosed with a specific illness covered by the policy.

However, you may have spotted the potential flaw in this insurance – you choose when it pays, for how long and how much.

As you would expect, the more you want to be paid, the sooner you want it and the longer you want to be paid for, the more the policy will cost you each month.

Therefore, this illustrates why it is important to properly consider implementing a set of insurance policies that complement one another to reduce the chance of you having to dip into savings or revert to credit cards when you are ill, thus keeping your Plan A on track.

What are you waiting for?

After acknowledging your Plan A and how easily it can be derailed, the simple question is, why aren't you taking action to protect it? After all, this is a situation where time is not your friend. The older you get, the more expensive your insurance is likely to cost, as it is based on your health at the point you apply for it. As we get older, we invariably pick up more aches, pains, knocks and strange skin tags. So, delaying insuring your health is also painful for your wallet.

Key points to remember
- Insurance is the first and MOST IMPORTANT step in building strong foundations for your Plan A, and to feel good about your money.
- Insure your most valuable asset and remember most people misidentify it.
- Your most valuable asset is your health. Without it your ability to earn an income is dramatically reduced.
- Just because you have health insurance doesn't mean you're in the clear.

- When choosing your policy, be careful to ensure that it will cover you for the events you are most likely to encounter during your working life
- This is a heavy chapter, but this is important stuff. There is no point in you reading any further without understanding the importance of health insurance.
- It gets more cheerful after this, I promise.

3 Emergency Fund

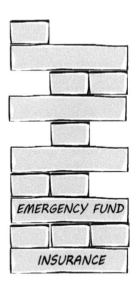

Create a pot before you need it

Bad things happen.

When they do, make sure you do not jeopardise your Plan A to pay for them.

Maslow re-enters Stage Left

In Maslow's theory, he talks about how we sometimes ignore the things that are necessary to keep us safe and happy, stating this is a weakness of humans.

Why? Because ...

- We can forget what it was like to struggle
- If we haven't struggled in a certain way before, we do not know what it is like and, therefore, do not make efforts to avoid it
- Sometimes we only feel the need for safety during an emergency, not before it

In short, Maslow is highlighting that we humans have a propensity to be negligent – when times are easy, we get lazy.

Yet, there are so many things that can derail our Plan A. Here is a list of things that many of us will have experienced:

- Ill health

- Accident
- Ill health or accident of a dependent family member (i.e. spouse, kids, parents or grandparents)
- Redundancy
- Recession
- Car accident (where you don't want to claim as the premiums will rocket)
- Car breaks down
- Boiler stops working
- Drain blockage
- Plumbing leak
- Roof leak
- Burglary
- Broken valuables, such as computer, phone, etc.

Yet, despite being aware of the ability of these issues to derail our Plan A, as Maslow identifies, we frequently do nothing until it's too late. This is where an emergency fund takes centre stage.

What is an emergency fund?

It's a pot of money kept in a current account, savings account or an equivalent cash pot. It is low risk, so you won't be earning much interest on it, and it will potentially be 'eroded by inflation' if the cost of living increases more quickly than the interest you earn on it.

However, it's easy to access without a financial penalty or worrying it is 'down' in value at the time of withdrawal, because it is not invested.

That being said, DO NOT touch it, unless it is in the event of an emergency.

What happens if you don't have an emergency fund?

Here are some of the horrible outcomes that can occur when you don't have an emergency fund to call upon during challenging times:

● Taking money from savings, which depletes them

● Dragging money out of investments, especially if they are down in value at the point you need them

● Exposing you and your family to not being able to pay your bills

● You may be forced into a position where you have to do something that you know is financially unhealthy, such as make purchases with a credit card, take out a loan or borrow money from family or friends

● Increased stress where it could have otherwise been avoided.

Right, so how big should your emergency fund be?

As a rule of thumb, your emergency fund should be a minimum of three times your monthly outgoings.

If you can, and would like extra points from Maslow and me, try and get to six times your monthly outgoings.

You could actually go as far as twelve times your monthly outgoings and beyond, if you are extremely risk averse.

However, beyond this point you could then make the argument that you are unnecessarily exposing your money to erosion by inflation (the cost of living increasing), and that your money could work harder if stored in other ways.

Upon assessing clients' finances, I frequently find that they have already amassed a sufficient emergency fund, although they may have not acknowledged it directly.

This scenario has both positives and negatives. Clearly, it is a positive that they have already built a sufficient emergency fund; so they are not vulnerable at this point in their financial tower.

However, it is a negative that they have not compartmentalised their emergency fund, as it could easily be eaten away over time, by either emergencies or general spending.

Therefore, it is important to acknowledge what value your emergency fund should be, and ensure it remains at that level, topping it up as needed.

For ease, many clients move their emergency fund to a bank account from which no direct debits are taken and for which no debit cards exist, so it is not exposed to depletion over time.

How big is Mark and Lisa's emergency fund, then?

Mark and Lisa enter Stage Right

Mark and Lisa's outgoings are £3,500 per month. Therefore, this is what their emergency fund could look like:

- 3x = £10,500
- 6x = £21,000
- 12x = £42,000

Let's put Mark and Lisa through another troublesome scenario they could feasibly face.

It's November and Mark and Lisa's boiler has stopped working, which is just typical as Mark was determined not to turn on the heating for as long as possible to save on bills (much to Lisa's delight), then it breaks after only a few uses, when the temperature outside has really started to drop!

To add insult to injury, the heating engineer is almost impossible to get hold of because lots of other people are realising their boilers have stopped working too. #AdultingSucks!

The boiler couldn't be fixed and needed replacing, which cost £3,000, plus another £2,000 for installation.

Then Mark's car got two punctures, and the tyres cost a further £300 to fix. Great!

As these sorts of things come in threes, somewhat like a law of physics, their youngest daughter suddenly needs to borrow some money (a deposit for a rental apartment), so that's an extra £1,500.

The 'bank of mum and dad' never officially closes, does it? That's a whopping £6,800 of unexpected costs.

#ThanksAdulting!

As Mark and Lisa have just paid for their summer holiday, they really didn't have the spare cash to cover all these unexpected costs.

And to add a cherry on top of this super-expensive cake, Christmas is around the corner, and they need to buy presents.

Mark and Lisa usually have around £10,000 between them in their current accounts, from which their income and bills go in and out. However, their holiday reduced that down to £3,000, so they had to dip into their savings to cover these unexpected costs. Before using their savings, they decided against two alternative options:

1) Credit cards

They didn't like the thought of potentially paying a high level of interest, as these unexpected outgoings would take more than a few months to pay off.

2) Lisa's Stocks and Shares ISA

Lisa's conundrum was that the investment markets were doing terribly and her money was down in value. She doesn't know much about investing, but she did know that taking money out whilst it's down is not a great idea as it will not have the opportunity to recover.

So, they used their savings.

Are Mark and Lisa's savings intended for these sorts of things? Heck, no!

They were intended to help with the second daughter's first home deposit. She is looking for properties at the moment and wants to put down a deposit in January. Brilliant timing!

Aside from money, the problems continue.

This entire situation is very stressful. Mark and Lisa end up having a couple of arguments; Mark is fed up with Lisa buying Christmas presents; Lisa is annoyed with Mark for insisting they go to the slightly nicer, and considerably more expensive, hotel for their holiday, turning something they were supposed to be looking forward to into a lingering anxiety-inducer.

They are also frustrated with having to shower at Mark's brother's house whilst the boiler is being fixed – they hesitated to get it fixed at first because Mark wanted to see if he could sort it out himself using YouTube (we all know how that turned out).

Now, this scenario may sound rather dramatic, but I have witnessed situations like this arise frequently over time.

In fact, it's a situation that pretty much everyone experiences in one way or another during their lifetime.

So, what's the solution? An emergency fund![2]

As I mentioned at the start, this book is all about helping you to recalibrate your relationship with money so that you can build strong foundations that keep your Plan A on track.

---

2 I appreciate this is a privileged position to be in, which is why we look at addressing it very early on, before you even consider investing.

Having insurance and an emergency fund in place is key to doing that.

Once you have those two things sorted, we can get into the fun bit – like investments …

Key points to remember

- Create an emergency fund *before* you need it.
- Your emergency fund should be a minimum of three times your monthly outgoings; six times gets you extra points; twelve times is superb, but inflation starts to become an issue.
- Not having an emergency fund can cause your financial health to take a dive very quickly.
- It also puts unnecessary pressure and strain on you and your relationships.
- An emergency fund needs to be in place before you even entertain the idea of investing your money.
- Having your insurance and emergency funds sorted means your financial foundations are stable enough to begin building investments on top.

4 Investing

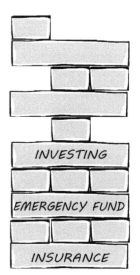

Now we have covered the most important parts of your financial tower (insurance and emergency fund), we can look at the bit most people want to know about when it comes to their finances ...

Investing!

I mentioned before that investing is usually people's go-to topic when they find out I'm a financial adviser, so I hope you're on the edge of your seat for this one.

Are you asking the wrong questions when it comes to investing?

Let's go back to Mark and Lisa for this.

Some of the first words that left Mark's mouth when initially talking to me about his finances were 'should I invest in cryptocurrency?'

Then, before I could reply, Mark's question was accompanied by a second: 'and how much should I invest each month?'

Mark's questions scared the heck out of me ...

Mark is an intelligent guy and a successful business owner, yet his questions were no more advanced than an inquisitive and impressionable apprentice's. And it's the thinking at the root of these sorts of questions that can have a destabilising impact on your financial tower.

As a result, in this chapter we will cover the questions you *should* be asking to get the most out of investing. Questions like:

- Can I afford to invest?
- How much should I invest?
- What should I invest in?

Before we move on, it's also important you know what *not* to expect from this chapter:

- Market predictions
- A list of the latest, hottest stocks to purchase
- An in-depth description of the different asset types.

It's not necessary to understand any of these points if, like Mark, you have not fully grasped the fundamentals of investing.

It's also irrelevant unless you are planning on quitting your job and becoming a DIY investment trader!

A tour guide to investing

Imagine you are visiting a city you don't know, where they don't speak your language, you can't grasp the exchange rate and your appearance is a pickpocket's dream. Wouldn't that be daunting? Instead, think of me as your tour guide to investing, and this chapter as the tour bus – I know the local language; I know the good places to eat; I know the neighbourhoods to avoid; I know the local customs; I can make sense of everything, so you can relax and focus on enjoying yourself.

So, all aboard the investment tour bus. Sounds fun, doesn't it?

First stop – Can you afford to invest?

As I explained via Mark's example, I frequently meet people who immediately ask me how much they should invest and where.

However, they are missing out a very important question: 'can they *afford* to invest?' As we covered in the previous chapters, this isn't a financial question, it's a question of preparedness. 'Can you afford to invest?' is asking whether you have built a sufficiently strong financial tower to cope with the strain that investing will put on it.

To make this question easier to answer, ask yourself these four simple questions …

1. Is the money you're looking to invest earmarked to spend on something specific?
2. Will you need it within five years?
3. Do you have loans (not including mortgages) or outstanding balances on credit cards?
4. Is your health still uninsured?

If you answered 'yes' to any of these questions, stop reading immediately (this is why I work in finance and not sales), go back to the start of the book, and complete the incomplete levels of your financial hierarchy of needs. Your financial tower is not stable enough to build upon at this point and doing so is likely to jeopardise your Plan A.

By all means, once you have done that continue reading to the end, advance to Go, collect £200, and feel free to leave me a nice review on Amazon.

You continued reading regardless, didn't you?

It's okay, I knew you would.

The reason why I asked you to go back isn't to sabotage my book reviews, but because so many people fail to take note of whether they can withstand the *risk* of investing, much like Mark.

I don't blame Mark though, in the same way that I don't blame you. Instead, I blame the fact that none of us were taught about the simple principles of money management at school.

We were not given the tools, or the assembly guide, to deal with these questions – more on this soon.

Before we progress any further on our tour, it's important to address a thought you might have had. Whilst reading this chapter, you might have wondered, 'surely savings should go in between emergency fund and investing?

Otherwise, I'll have no savings, right?' Wrong. This is another sign that we aren't taught about money at school.

Looking at things from this perspective will help: you *do* have savings, just look back at the answers you gave to the question 'Can you afford to invest?' These are your savings. The point here is that too much emphasis is placed on saving money and not enough attention is given to the emergency fund and investments below and above it. Therefore, the intention here is to make sure you aren't saving too much. You read that correctly – to make sure you aren't saving too much.

During times of low inflation (the rate at which the cost of living gradually increases), this statement might seem crazy.

However, during times of high inflation this point makes much more sense. If you save more money than you have earmarked for expenditure within the next five years, you are essentially giving large amounts of it away, because when the rate of inflation is higher than the interest you receive on your savings, the amount of goods and services your savings can purchase is reducing over time.

So, whilst reducing your focus on savings and increasing the attention you pay to your emergency fund and investing isn't necessarily intended to make your financial tower more stable, it is designed to prevent you from that horrible habit many people adopt – working hard to save money, just to see it eroded by the silent winds of inflation. Once you have amassed your emergency fund, if you don't need whatever is in excess of that amount within five years, invest it!

Second stop – How much should you invest?

This question seems to confuse or completely overwhelm people. Again, that's not anyone's fault. School does not provide us with the skills to answer this question.

There are various unhelpful answers to this question.

I have read far too many books that give very specific descriptions of the percentage of income you should give to different areas of your finances.

For example: 'spend 50% now, then put 20% into a savings account, invest 20% and give 10% to a charity of your choice'.

This kind of advice is about as useful as your GP providing you with a prescription before you've even entered their office!

Instead, here is a metaphor that will help you consider how much you should invest. Think about exercise and going to the gym.

Let's say you've gone to the gym – massive kudos to you because that is a mental battle in itself!

When you are at the gym on the treadmill, if you barely put in enough effort to raise your heart rate and break a sweat, you shouldn't expect to see many improvements in the future, right?

Now, if on that treadmill you have increased your heart rate, elevated your breathing and can feel your muscles gulping down lactic acid, you can then expect to see some results that will put a smile on your face in the future. Still agree?

Then again, if on that same treadmill, you are holding on for dear life, knuckles whitening as you grip the safety rails, feeling like your heart is about to pop out of your chest and a rattlesnake has plunged its fangs into your Achilles tendon, you have probably taken things too far. Still with me?

By pushing too hard, you have probably injured yourself and will need to stop to recover for a few weeks. Your training has been derailed, you will likely see your hard-earned physical results diminish, in (annoyingly) half the time it took to achieve them, and it will be some time until you are back in condition again, let alone thinking about improving upon it.

Let's break down these varying treadmill situations:

- The lazy gym-goer is the equivalent of not putting enough into your investments
- The hard-working gym-goer is the equivalent of putting enough into your investments
- And the Mo Farah wannabe gym-goer is the equivalent of putting in too much.

Now, this may all seem like a convenient way of not providing percentages for the amount you should contribute to your investments. However, everyone's circumstances, and therefore their finances, are completely different.

So, this approach relies upon your knowledge of your own finances to ensure you contribute an amount appropriate for you.

Like exercise, this analogy shows you that not putting enough into your investments, instead preferring to spend your money on yourself now, is absolutely fine and will make you feel better in the short-term.

However, do not expect to have a big smile on your face in the future, when your investments look anaemic.

Likewise, contributing too much will hurt in the event you have to take some out at short notice because you are at the mercy of fluctuations in the value of your investments.

This means you could lose money if your investments are down in value, as it will take away their chance to recover.

Therefore, the best amount to put in is the amount that feels ever so slightly uncomfortable (like being out of breath and feeling lactic acid in your muscles).

In other words, put yourself in a position where you feel the contributions as a slight sacrifice each month, but not an offering to the gods! That way, you will be much happier with the health of your investments in the future.

Much like 'you are what you eat', your investments will be what you contribute.

Third stop – what should you invest in?

Much as I was not overly prescriptive about how much you should invest, I am not going to give you a low-down on the hottest stocks to invest in.

I will avoid taking you on a wild and immersive safari through the different asset types, as that in itself would not be a book, but an entire series. Instead, I think it is important that you are equipped with a net and a bat.

'A net and a bat? What kind of crazy tour bus is this?!' I hear you whisper to the person next to you.

Think of it like this …

When you are out in the world, you are bombarded by friends, colleagues, the man down the pub, TV adverts and social media posts each proclaiming to have the best performing investment for you.

Therefore, it is far more useful for you to put into your investment toolkit a net, to catch the opportunities that you don't want to miss out on, and a bat, to smack away those that will not help you.

Knowing whether to use the net or the bat

How do you decide which tool is best for the job? To help you determine whether an investment is any good, see how many points it ticks in the list below …

1. Does it go up in value over time?
2. Does it provide an income in the meantime?
3. Do you understand it fully?
4. Is it low cost to maintain?
5. Can it be easily withdrawn when needed?

Let's break down those points …

1) Does it go up in value over time?

You would hope the answer to this question is yes, as this is the principal aim of investing – for your money to go up in value within a specific time period. Simple.

2) Does it provide an income in the meantime?

It's always great for an investment to pay you for owning it. Plus, there's usually a cost for owning an investment, so this helps take care of that. For example, just think about the following investments – what is the likelihood of them paying you an income whilst owning them?

- Car – unlikely, unless you lease it out (brave)
- Racehorse – only if it's fast (fingers crossed)

- Investment portfolio – if you have invested in income-producing assets, yes
- Gold – nope (unless you rent it out for rap music videos)
- Property – yes, via rent (but only when tenants reside in it).

3) Do you understand it fully?

Right, this is crunch time. Can you clearly explain the asset, out loud, to other people, whilst making sense and not sensationalising it, or sticking up for it?

The importance of this is simple. If I said to you, 'give me £100 and I will put it into a hole that I have dug in the ground. Then, in five years, when we take the money out it will have grown to £5,000. Deal?'

No deal! You would probably tell me to get lost, using a few carefully selected and impolite words, as that makes no sense and sounds like a terrible idea.

So, why do you consider putting your money into other things that either make no sense or sound silly, or both?

As Warren Buffett, probably the greatest contemporary investor, once said, 'Long ago, Sir Isaac Newton gave us three laws of motion, which were the work of genius. Unfortunately, Sir Isaac's talents didn't extend to investing.

Sir Isaac Newton lost a bundle in the South Sea Bubble, explaining later, "I can calculate the movement of the stars, but not the madness of men".'

'DAMN IT! I GIVE UP!'

'I CAN'T BE BOTHERED FINDING THE
FOURTH LAW OF MOTION NOW, I'M SKINT!'

4) Is it low cost to maintain?

Let's use the examples mentioned above:

- Car – has maintenance, storage and insurance costs
- Racehorse – will need feeding, housing, transporting
- Investment portfolio – annual management charge, ongoing advice charge, early withdrawal charge, product charge
- Gold – cost of keeping it in a safe location
- Property – maintenance, repairs, cleaning between tenants, insurance, paying mortgage for periods without tenants.

5) Can it be easily withdrawn when needed?

Accessing your money when you need it is crucial. This can be for planned events, such as when you have reached the point in time when you want to finally spend the money.

Or it could be for something more spontaneous (not forgetting that you would use your emergency fund to take care of emergencies).

Regardless of the scenario that tempts you to withdraw the money, it is important to understand whether you can access it with minimal fuss when needed.

Evidently, the more of the five questions above you can answer 'yes' to, the more likely it is you can use the net. Conversely, the more questions you answer 'no' to, the more likely it is you will need to reach for the bat.

If you answer 'don't know' to any question, it can mean one of two things:

1. You should avoid it, or …
2. You should learn more about it.

To ensure you are doing what is best for your financial tower, it is wise to compare different investments as it will highlight their respective strengths and weaknesses. For example: gold, cryptocurrency, a house, shares, whisky, cars, even a racehorse … they're all investments! Some will tick more boxes than others; some will require the net; some will deserve the bat.

Now, when I asked Mark to consider these five questions regarding his interest in cryptocurrency, he quickly found he couldn't answer 'yes' to many of them. As a result, he didn't need any convincing from me on cryptocurrency's appropriateness for his needs, as he could easily determine whether it would keep him on track to reach his Plan A destination, or not.

Where to next, on this tour? Let's stretch our legs

'Ladies and gentlemen, I hope you have enjoyed the sights thus far on our journey through the rolling hills of investing. At this point in the trip, we will now disembark from the bus, stretch our legs and take a stroll around some of the myth-ical attractions the investing landscape has to offer' (I announce in my best tour-guide voice, that strange tone also used by flight attendants, as though they are pinching their nose whilst talking).

The rest of this chapter is aimed at helping you think about investing in a constructive way – a way that will not lead you to take crazy decisions, lose all your money and bring your Plan A to a grinding halt.

As your tour guide to investing, this includes showing you how not to be your own worst enemy.

And I will do so by heroically busting a series of seven myths, as the investment world is riddled with them!

Myth 1 – We are talking about the same thing

Are you thinking about speculating, saving or investing?

I ask because these three things are very different, yet many people see them as the same thing.

Here's an overview of the definitions:

- Speculating is like putting a bet on a racehorse in the Grand National

- Saving is what we covered in an earlier chapter, where we went over your emergency fund, then put aside money you had earmarked for expenditure or knew you would spend within the next five years

- Investing is the process of putting your money into specifically identified assets for a predetermined time frame so, at the point you wish to spend it, it is higher in value than before you started.

Speculators are, in effect, gambling. They are trying to predict whether investment markets will go up or down, left or right, then take a decision that is the opposite from the herd and, subsequently, make their money grow.

The flaw with this approach is that you are trying to predict circumstances largely outside of your control. However, if you could speculate with such mastery, people would copy you and eventually move in the same direction as you, stripping away your competitive advantage.

That said, if you want to speculate, that's absolutely fine, just don't do it with your investable money. When I initially meet clients, they frequently have some money in shares of companies they have hand-picked.

They ask me what they should do with them, since they are taking my advice on the other areas of their finances. In response, I often tell them to continue, as long as it's an amount that will not reduce them to tears if they lose it.

It can be healthy to take an interest in different companies around the world, assess their business strategy and guess whether the future will be kind to them or not.

You could argue this is a good way of keeping on top of current affairs. Yet, my only caution is to not contribute any more than you would when betting on the Grand

National, as that is, in essence, what you are doing – gambling.

Myth 2 – 'I don't want to invest because I don't want to take risks with my money'

Well, for starters, there is no such thing as 'zero risk' when taking decisions with your money.

Granted, some places to invest your money are riskier than others, but risk is ever-present.

There's a risk in not investing.

Let's use Mark as an example for this.

Mark stated he did not want to invest, as he wished to avoid taking risks with his and Lisa's money.

This is understandable. Investing can be scary. We're not taught about it in school and there is lots of confusing and contradictory information out there.

However, when making this statement, Mark did not consider the risk of doing nothing.

By doing nothing, and leaving his money in the bank, Mark would expose himself to other risks, such as:

- Low interest rates
- Inflation
- Bank failure.

Risk in investing is something that needs to be embraced rather than feared.

Once you have accepted that there is no decision you

can take with your money that doesn't include a degree of risk, it is paramount that you grasp this next point: investment risk should be embraced, not feared.

Embracing risk does not mean that it disappears, it just means you are aware of it, understand it and do not react to it negatively.

After all, risk is the reason investments grow. I'll say that again: *risk is the reason investments grow.*

The majority of people reading this book will be British, so will understand that we live on a rather drizzly little island. For those of you who are not British, you will understand that we live on a rather drizzly little island because of the jokes you have likely heard (or told).

The sketch above shows something we are all familiar with – plants need rain to grow.

Do we enjoy rain? Not really. Is it essential for the growth of plants and food? Absolutely.

Therefore, in order to invest successfully (and happily), it's wise to reacquaint yourself with risk. After all, it cannot be avoided, therefore it must be embraced.

For Mark, this was an eye-opener. I went a step further to cement this thought in Mark's mind:

When it comes to investing there *will* be seasons, just as there are in nature. There will be summer and winter.

There will be seasons you like more than others. Regardless, the seasons are necessary for the plants that grow in their particular environment. It can't be summer all the time, unless you want to live in a desert!

Myth 3 – You are perfectly rational

On the open plains of Africa, when a herd of zebras (also known as a zeal) see grass moving in a suspicious way, one will sound a series of piercing screeches and the entire zeal will bolt to safety.

The zebras do not wait to see if a lion is present before bolting, as that would be too late. They bolt because they believe they have seen a pattern that constitutes a lion's presence (grass moving + alarm screech = leg it!).

They all bolt at the same time because there is safety in numbers. The evolution of the zebras' genetics is keeping them alive.

Now, given that most of the time there is probably no lion present, you could argue the zebras are being over-zeal-ous (get it?), but this has kept them alive to date, so who are we to argue with them? (I will stop with the zebra analogy before you mistake me for Sir David Attenborough.)

We humans, like zebras, have also evolved to spot patterns and move with the herd for safety. Therefore, when we see a drop in the value of our investments, we are preconditioned to acknowledge the pattern and dart toward a more secure position.

When you see a drop in your investments this is exactly what is happening – you've observed a seemingly threatening pattern, a large number of people are withdrawing their money from a particular investment asset simultaneously and, as a result, the value of that company reduces to reflect its decreasing popularity.[3]

Our instinctive, primitive reaction to investment patterns that appear negative is a very quick way of losing our money.

At this point, I think it's about time for another sketch to help me explain this …

Now more than ever we are bombarded with a constant stream of 'information', via 24/7 news, social media, television, podcasts, etc. Yet, we do not take notice of it all.

3 For investment nerds, please note that this description has very much been oversimplified for the purpose of explaining things in a swift and light manner. If you don't like it, find another zeal to hang out with.

For example, we are exposed to hundreds of adverts each day on our mobile phones alone, urging us to buy the latest health supplement because it will make us immortal, or an upgraded smartphone with voice recognition that actually works (just imagine).

As a result of all these adverts, do we purchase the items? Absolutely not! In fact, when you think about the volume of adverts we are exposed to, we actually buy very few items as a proportion.

This is because we ignore a lot of the useless information: we sift through the things that are not helpful whatsoever, we reject the topics that are not applicable to us, and we take on board the miniscule amount of feedback that will *actually* benefit us.

A tangible sign of when a piece of useless information has snuck through your filter is when you end up with a useless piece of plastic, usually purchased from Amazon, that you only use once because you never really needed it.

So, why don't you apply that same trash filter when it comes to useless information about investments?

Ignorance is genuinely bliss here.

When you look at the news and there is a detailed story depicting how squillions of pounds and dillions of dollars have been lost from the FTSE 100 and the S&P 500, whilst professional investors are pictured frantically heckling on investment floors, it sends panic shooting through your spine.

You have seen a pattern, and not a good one. You look at what the rest of the herd are doing and they're scampering to safety. What do you do? You follow the herd. In effect, your natural human instincts have kicked in. In most other situations this impulse would have kept you alive. In this situation, however, it could have lost you a lot of money.

How do we fix this? By choosing what to ignore.

Another sketch? Why not?

This sketch is actually a smoothed-out version of a real graph, containing real data. The original graph displays the performance of the world's biggest companies between 1990 and 2022.[4]

However, I promised that we are not going to delve into the minutiae of investment detail as, unless you are intending to quit your job and make it your primary source of income, you don't need to.

---

4 Again, for those investment nerds, the graph reflects the MSCI (Morgan Stanley Capital International) World Index. In plain English, this means the graph is intended to show the performance of large and medium company shares in over 20 developed countries. It covers the majority of the world's largest companies and, therefore, is a good gauge for investment performance across the globe.

After all, there's nothing worse than a tour guide who rambles on about irritatingly microscopic features whilst visiting a colossal wonder of the world.

Perspective is paramount for safe and successful investing. When you focus in on the teeny tiny up and down fluctuations of investments it is enough to make you feel sick, like going on an erratic rollercoaster.

Investments are valued by the minute, which is brilliant if you are making decisions by the minute. But, when you are making plans that span years, even decades, into the future, including key life stages such as retirement, this level of magnification on investment value movements provides you with far too much detail.

This is why reacting to daily news on investments is overexposing you to useless information and is conducive to overzealous reactions. I agree, it takes a lot to go against your human instinct to flee to safety, but zooming out from minute-by-minute detail will increase your confidence in the health of your investments.

In the sketch on the previous page, when you look at the zoomed-out line, it is much smoother, and you can recognise a more positive trajectory over time. In contrast, when you look at the zoomed-in line, it is much more volatile, and you cannot tell whether its next move will be up or down.

Further still, liken these two lines to your mood when looking at them – one is smoother and more positive, the other is more volatile and uncertain. Which journey would you rather take? Which person would you rather be? There *is* a choice.

It starts with drowning out useless information, which is achieved by stepping back and panicking less. Humans move with the herd; that's part of our nature.

Investments go up and down; that's part of their nature. This is a terrible mix of natural traits if you act upon instinct alone. Calm is the key. Better yet, sanguine is the key (plus, it sounds more like sangria).

> I LIKE SANGUINE, IT TASTES LOVELY!

Myth 4 – A year is a long time

A year might seem like a long time in *your* life, but it's not a long time in investing.

When it comes to investing, a year is a very short period.

In fact, 5–10 years is classed as a short-term investment; 10–15 years is a medium-term investment; over 15 years is a long-term investment.

In investment terms, the professional investment managers buying and selling your stocks and shares will, themselves, have strategies spanning long time horizons. Therefore, dipping your money into their funds or portfolios for a short period is like getting off a train at the stop *before* the one you actually want to get off at.

It makes no sense and is a waste of your time and money!

Myth 5 – 'But, the news says I've lost all my money'

Well, if the news has said it, it must be true … Yeah, right!

Then again, it does feel scary when you hear on the news that the world's finances are plummeting. Especially when you have as much control over them as a helter-skelter …

So, the next time the news has you sobbing into your pillow after proclaiming 'Newsflash: Hysteria on Wall Street, as stock markets tumble uncontrollably', just ask yourself this question: has there been an apocalypse?

Conceivably, what event would have to take place for global investment markets to drop to the extent that you lose all of your money, and for it to never recover?

Seriously, just think about that for a moment – what would it take for you to lose all of your money irrevocably?

Well, if you are speculating, not much. Simply the company, or companies, you have chosen to invest in go bust. That's it. Money gone.

However, if your money is invested in a wide range of companies, across a vast selection of industries, in varying countries throughout the world, the situation is very different indeed!

All those companies, or at least the vast majority, would have to go bust for you to lose your money without recovery. You'll agree, there's far less likelihood of that irreversible event happening to a large group of companies in different countries, as their trading performance will not be sensitive to the same economic and political forces. Therefore, the next time you hear a news anchor state that investment markets are in jeopardy, just remember, if your investment eggs are in different baskets, something apocalyptic would have to happen for you to lose all your money. Not to mention – if there was an apocalypse, your investments would probably be the least of your worries!

Myth 6 – 'My investment has gone down. This is terrible news!'

Once Mark had reacquainted himself with risk, it was important for him to reframe his understanding of drops in the value of investment markets.

Drops in investment markets are reported in the news as catastrophic events because, as you know, bad news sells. However, this is predominantly entertainment.

If drops in the market are viewed from an educational perspective instead, they take on a whole new meaning.

I explained this to Mark as follows …

Me: 'Where do you do your weekly shopping?'

Mark: 'Tesco', he replied, grinning, yet clearly restraining himself from saying, 'where on earth are you going with this?'

Me: 'OK. Do you drink tea or coffee?'

Mark: 'Coffee'.

Me: 'What brand of coffee do you drink?'

Mark: 'I like the Cost-a-Lot coffee pods that go in my coffee machine'.

Me: 'I see, nice choice. Now, imagine this: when you go into Tesco and arrive at the aisle where the Cost-a-Lot coffee pods are shelved, quite often you will find that they are discounted by, say 50%, right?'

Mark: 'Yes, that happens quite a lot, actually'.

Me: 'And, when that happens, what do you do?'

Mark: 'I buy more than one, of course!', he asserted presumptuously.

Me: 'Exactly! Me too, in fact. So, how would you feel if I said your investment had dropped in value?'

Mark: 'Well, it would usually make me feel really anxious, but I can see where you're going with this now'.

Much like resisting the urge to move with the herd, understanding and implementing the lesson from this next sketch is much easier said than done. Nevertheless, it is a cornerstone for successful investing.

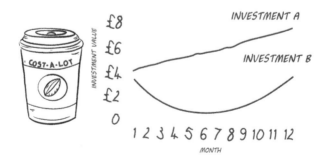

Generally, when it comes to money, we have been conditioned to think that 'down is bad' and 'up is good'.

And who can blame us? If you go onto your online banking app and see that your savings have gone down since you last looked at them, that's bad news because your savings should be accruing interest and going up in value slowly.

Therefore, if you open an investment app and see that your investment has gone down in value, you wouldn't be criticised for thinking that that is an equally bad trend to see.

However, the two things you are comparing (savings and investments) are different things entirely.

This is why we have been conditioned to think that investment 'A' in this sketch will give us with greater investment growth than investment 'B'.

However, unlike your savings, investments have the ability to benefit from decreasing in value, especially if you are contributing to them periodically.

Let's shine a light on why.

Firstly, swap the words 'shares in a company' for 'units'.

If you have decided to buy units in, for example, Cost-a-Lot Coffee, contributing £10 per month, the cost of those units would determine how many units your £10 could purchase each month.

In the illustration, in month 1, the units cost £4 for both investments A and B, so your £10 will buy equal amounts of each investment.

By month 7, investment A's units have increased in value to £6.33, meaning your £10 will purchase fewer units than it did in month 1.

On the other hand, investment B's units have decreased to £0.75 by month 7, meaning your £10 will buy more units than it did in month 1.

At this point, if you owned investment B, you could be forgiven for panicking and thinking that you picked the wrong horse. However, we are considering investments, not savings, so the outcome will go against our human instincts.

By month 12, if you were to look at the lines that represent the performance of investment A in comparison to investment B, you would think that the value of investment A's units had gone up the most.

Well, you would be right. Investment A's units *have* increased from £4 to £8, whilst investment B's decreased from £4 to £2, then recovered back to £4.

However, if you thought that investment A would be valued higher than investment B after 12 months, you would be wrong.

The owner of investment B would have the biggest smile on their face, as the cumulative value of their units is higher than the value of those belonging to investment A.

Here's why: investment A purchased 20 units during the 12-month period, valued at £165 in month 12. However, investment B purchased 83 units, valued at £334 in month 12. There you have it. In the same way that Mark buys more Cost-a-Lot coffee pods when they're on discount at Tesco, a very similar mechanism is at play when considering investments.

Myth 7 – 'The best investment is the one that grows the most, right?'

Now that we have solved the debate as to whether bigger is better (well, in investment terms at least), we are well-equipped to tackle the final investment myth.

Let's throw another sketch into the mix to give us the drive we need to finish our investment myth-busting extravaganza.

The two cars being compared are an American muscle car (top) and a Formula 1 Grand Prix car (bottom), both of which are renowned for going from A to B very quickly.

On the one hand, you may be familiar with the unit of measurement for engines being litres – the more litres, the bigger the engine. Generally speaking, we assume the bigger the engine, the faster the car.

On the other hand, you might be less certain about the meaning of horsepower

EFFICIENCY

~~GROWTH~~ IS THE KEY TO INVESTING

5 LITRE ENGINE (RISK)
450 HORSEPOWER (GROWTH)

1·6 LITRE ENGINE (RISK)
1,050 HORSEPOWER (GROWTH)

(I swear, I am going somewhere constructive with this metaphor, just bear with me).

Horsepower was initially used as a measurement in the 18th century to compare the difference in power between the new transport being introduced at the time (steam trains) and the old version that preceded them (horses).

They were literally showing the power of the steam train by showing how many horses it would take to develop the same level of power (I'd love to see that experiment!). Needless to say, more horsepower = more powerful engine; more powerful engine = faster car.

So, if you look at the size of the muscle car engine (5 litres), you might think, 'why don't Formula 1 drivers use muscle cars instead, as their engines are much bigger?'

However, the determining factor of a car's speed is horsepower, *not* litres. And, as the stats in the illustration show, the Formula 1 car crams far more stallions under the bonnet than the muscle car! Therefore, you could say that, as the Formula 1 car produces more power with a smaller engine. It is more efficient.

Growth is not the be all and end all.

What's the point in this crazy ramble? Growth is not necessarily the most important element in investing. Instead, it is useful to think of efficiency as the key ingredient, especially if you want to preserve the stability of your financial tower.

Just think of it like this: if engine size (litres) is risk, then horsepower is growth. Therefore, if I offer you two investments, both providing similar levels of growth, how do you compare which is most suitable for you? Well, you could ask, 'which one is taking the most risk to achieve that growth?'

If one investment is taking a monumental amount of risk to produce a similar amount of reward as another investment, it could be considered less efficient with the risk it is taking. Hence, efficiency is the key to investing whilst staying on track to make your Plan A a reality.

Key points to remember

- Can you afford to invest? Consider your insurance and emergency fund first.
- Knowing how much to invest is completely personal to you, but it should make you feel like you are trying hard on a treadmill – uncomfortable, but good for you in the long run.
- To know what you should invest in, you need a net and a bat – to catch useful information and wallop away the rest.
- Saving, speculating and investing are *not* the same thing.
- Where there is money, there is risk. Understanding and embracing risk is fundamental when it comes to successful (and happy) investing.
- Investing often means going against your natural instincts – and that's okay.
- It is oxymoronic to make decisions based on the day-to-day movement of your investments when you are playing the long game.

- Unless there's been an apocalypse, you probably haven't lost all your money (despite what the news says).
- Unlike your savings, investments can benefit from decreasing in value when you are contributing periodically.
- Efficiency is the key to investing, not growth.

5 Retirement

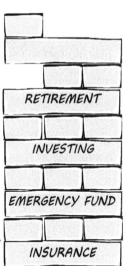

RETIREMENT

INVESTING

EMERGENCY FUND

INSURANCE

Before we get into this chapter, let's get the 'P' word out of the way nice and early.

The 'P' word is the first word that usually pops into someone's head when thinking about retirement. However, a 'P' isn't the only tool that will help you to achieve your retirement goals.

Now, I appreciate we humans can be creatures of habit. So, instead of trying to completely eliminate the 'P' word, let's instead replace it with another, far more accurate, word for describing what retirement is all about ... planning.

(For clarity, the previous 'P' word was pension).

No doubt you will be relieved to know this chapter is not going to be all about pensions and tax. After all, the purpose of this book is to help you prioritise; to forget about competing with your friends, family, colleagues and neighbours, and to focus on making *plans* on solid foundations to build a sturdy financial tower.

So, diving into pensions and tax would be counterintuitive, not to mention mind-numbing.

The importance of planning

Instead, this chapter is all about how to plan for retirement (see, there's our alternative 'P' word in action already). I will share with you the lessons I have learned from witnessing clients plan for, approach, enter and exit retirement.

Mark and Lisa, you're up!

Mark and Lisa's main priority was retiring at age 60, as the thought of working until their state pension age, 67, made them feel physically exhausted and, frankly, nauseous.

They thought 67 sounded too old to retire and felt they would not have enough energy to tick items off their bucket list. To recap, Mark and Lisa's version of retirement included:

- A couple of holidays per year
- A car each on Personal Contract Purchase (PCP), renewing it every three years
- Financially supporting their daughters with remaining university costs, first home deposits and weddings
- Looking after their grandchildren
- Selling their Buy-To-Let property and using the money to buy a little holiday home by the sea in Wales.

Yet, despite Mark and Lisa's firm feelings about retiring at age 60, they hadn't done much to make it happen.

They had, in effect, set out a lovely image for their future selves during retirement, but were using little more than hoping upon a miracle to ensure it came true.

Whilst age 60 used to sound like a long time away, now they are approaching 50 it suddenly seems alarmingly close. Hence, Mark and Lisa desperately needed a plan, as they didn't want to be too old to enjoy their bucket-list items. So, how do you plan for retirement?

What is retirement?

Retirement is *not* a challenge of wealth; it is a challenge of health. Just as people make assumptions about the future when starting off at the bottom of their financial tower, they also insert assumptions toward the top, when thinking about retirement.

TRAVELLING AFTER STATE PENSION AGE

WOULD YOU LIKE A WERTHER'S, YOUNG SIRS?

It is all well and good making plans for retirement – but if you are too old, knackered and skint to enjoy it, making plans is pointless.

It appears the answer to the question 'what is retirement?' has changed. In the not-too-distant past, retirement simply meant ceasing to work another day of your life.

This point was often determined by the age at which your state or company pension kicked in and reflected, rather depressingly, the mortality rates of the time.

However, we have come a long way since then, especially in terms of understanding the importance of our mental health when it comes to our decision to retire.

Stopping work entirely now seems to be a very unhealthy thing to do; your mental cogs soon become rusty and eventually seize up, plunging the owner into feeling a lack of purpose and, sometimes, depression. In this instance, many people return to what they know – work.

But what if there was a better way?

In my opinion, retirement is the art of doing more of the things you enjoy and fewer of the things you don't enjoy.

I'll say that again: *doing more of the things you enjoy and fewer of the things you don't enjoy*. Sounds lovely, right?

In essence, it is freedom of choice. You work bloody hard for a long time to earn that freedom, so it's worthwhile putting a plan in place to make sure your future freedom becomes a reality.

When I speak to clients about what their version of retirement looks like, they frequently mention the following:

- Providing more support for their children
- Seeing more of their grandchildren
- Gardening
- Walking
- Cycling
- Swimming

- Yoga
- Raising money for charity
- Learning to play a musical instrument
- Beginning a passion-project
- Sometimes starting another business! This time, with fewer hours and more enjoyment, oh, and not *needing* a profit to pay the bills!

However, clients seldom consider what is needed from them (not their finances) to enjoy their retirement wish list, such as the following:

- Energy
- Good mental health
- A functioning brain (especially considering the prevalence of dementia, Parkinson's and Alzheimer's)
- Healthy joints
- Balance
- Coordination
- People to enjoy their time with.

Can you see now that to enjoy retirement, not only will you need to have enough money, but you will also need to have good health.

Changing your mindset when it comes to retirement

We have all encountered a story, either first-hand or otherwise, where someone retires from work then, within a very short amount of time, either their health rapidly declines, or they pass away.

It is as though their body, upon its last day of work, gives a sigh of relief, and believes it's no longer required. This is very close to home for me.

Last year, at the time of writing, my dad, aged 66, suffered a stroke.

One day he was fine, rattling off dad jokes by the bucketload (which might explain a lot about the bad puns in this book), the next he was in and out of consciousness and slurring his words, somewhat resembling the way he is after one too many whiskies.

He had a bleed on the brain and the family were told to prepare for the worst. Again, he was age 66. His state pension had started only months previous, as had other pensions he was entitled to at that age. However, his body took no notice of that piece of information.

For many people, this would have been their first few months of retirement. Just imagine that.

Working from age 16 to age 66 – 50 years of toil. Then, your reward? Death. Great! Hence, planning to make the most out of your retirement is extremely important.

Luckily, my dad chose to retire at age 57. Even more fortunately, the bleed drained away into a part of the brain that allowed him to make a full recovery – although it hasn't cured the terrible dad jokes.

The moral of this story, however, is not necessarily to retire as early as humanly possible. Instead, it is to *plan* your retirement.

These are two very different things.

For example, in their fifties, my dad and step-mum were working five or six days a week to pay a large mortgage, which was due to be paid off when they were about 68.

They felt trapped by this. They would either have to work beyond the point their pensions kicked in at age 66 or work even more hours to make overpayments on their mortgage to retire sooner. Once they decided that this was not the version of retirement they wanted, they made a plan so that they could retire at age 57.

The plan consisted of selling the house, buying a canal boat and living on that for four to five years, whilst they toured the UK's 2,000 or so miles of canals (and many more thousands of canal-side pubs).

Then, they would sell the boat and purchase a house on dry land again, and use some of the left-over cash to purchase a caravan, in which they would tour the UK's thousands of caravan sites.

They didn't retire on a huge budget. Up to and during their retirement, my dad and step-mum have had to watch their pennies very closely.

Each step has been meticulously planned to ensure it is affordable and sustainable. Yet, they're not particularly financially savvy.

They never worked in the finance industry or had a formal education in money. Instead, it was important to them to enjoy retirement whilst they were healthy enough to do so, and they identified a plan was needed to make that happen. The point is, they are living a version of retirement that makes them extremely happy.

Moreover, even when my dad suffered a stroke, he had already experienced nine years of adventure.

Again, you don't need a pension, you need a plan (of which a pension may be a part).

So, how do you make a plan for retirement?

Good question. I'm glad you asked. I'm frequently asked, 'how much do I need to retire?'

Now, I have read numerous articles providing the reader with a range of figures that represent different levels of comfort and standard of living during retirement, much like descriptions of mattresses. In fact, the mattress descriptions are probably more useful for planning retirement.

From what I can gather, these figures have been plucked pretty much from thin air:

- £17,000 per couple per year for a 'minimum' standard of living in retirement
- £31,000 for 'moderate'
- £50,000 for 'comfortable'.

Whilst at first glance this might appear useful, I argue that these figures are more noise than information. I rarely find a client able to use them as the foundation for a retirement plan, as they do not know how each of the assets they own can be used to provide these levels of income during retirement.

Moreover, my dad and step-mum, by the above definition, are living on the 'minimum' amount per year, but would refer to their retirement as being on the 'comfortable' end of the spectrum: very contented, with almost no stress.So, instead of asking the question 'how much do I need to retire?' and using that as the end point for your plan, use this as the *starting* point, from which you create a retirement plan.

The following is an illustration of how this worked with Mark and Lisa.

1) What age do you want to retire and WHY?

- Age 60
- Because Mark and Lisa's parents both passed away around 70, so they feel working to age 67 will not leave them enough time and health to enjoy retirement

+

2) What do you want to do when you are retired?

- A couple of holidays per year
- A car each
- See daughters and look after grandchildren

+

3) How much do you need to fund that lifestyle?

- £21,600 per year (£1,800 per month)

X

4) How long will you live?

- Well, who can answer this question?!
- UK Office of National Statistics: Mark = age 84 average life expectancy, with a 25% chance of living to age 93
- UK Office of National Statistics: Lisa = age 87 average life expectancy, with a 25% chance of living to age 99

=

5) How much do you need to retire …?

- Therefore, Mark could be retired around 35 years, and Lisa 38 years
- Let's call that an average retirement of 36.5 years

=

£788,400 required for Mark and Lisa's retirement (36.5 x £21,600).

Mark and Lisa audibly gasped when they saw the resulting figure.

You might also look at the figure of £788,400 and think, 'brilliant, now what?' Worse still, you might look at the figure, consider it unachievable, then bury your head in the sand in the belief that you'll need to work until you drop dead. This is why this figure is the *starting* point for making a plan, *not* the end.

What to do now?

Firstly, look at the money that is coming your way, whether you like it or not. I call this, 'the money you can't avoid' (one of the nicest sources of money, if you ask me).

For example, in Mark and Lisa's case they are entitled to the full state pension at age 67, which, at the time of writing (2023), is £9,627.80 per year each, or £19,255.60 for them both.

So, if they wanted to retire at age 60, they would be footing the gap for the first 7 years, then their state pensions would kick in, making things much easier.

Mark and Lisa instantly found this a huge relief, that they wouldn't need to cough-up hundreds of thousands of pounds in order to even contemplate retiring.

Moreover, I asked Mark and Lisa, 'do you really think you will continue the same lifestyle right throughout retirement?'

Mark and Lisa then proceeded to explain to me that they expect that as their health and energy declines over time, so will their outgoings.

They also mentioned that they would not be able to travel to the holiday home in Wales forever, so that would eventually be sold, giving them an influx of cash to use during retirement. Further still, they mentioned that they would eventually become too old to live in their current house, as the stairs, cleaning and general accessibility would become too hard to navigate in their old age.

So, again, they would downsize, releasing more equity that they could use to fund their retirement. Even further, as they get older, their daughters will become less reliant upon them, they might have less need for two cars and, as a result, their monthly outgoings would decrease again.

Then, their two holidays abroad each year will eventually turn into holidays in the UK ... you get the point – they will spend less as they get older and release equity from different assets, which will add to the funds they live upon during retirement.[5]

---

5 Releasing equity from assets, such as downsizing a property, is mentioned by many clients as though it can be done with relative ease and low risk. However, let me be clear, this can be fraught with danger, so it is super-duper important to take advice when considering incorporating this into your plans..

This comes down to four points:

1. Remember the money that you can't avoid (many people forget to take this into account).
2. Your spending is likely to reduce throughout retirement.
3. You are able to downsize assets, such as property, during retirement to fund your outgoings.
4. Mark and Lisa were providing the answers without being prompted!

That's that for retirement, folks.

When it comes to retirement, I think it's crucial to keep things simple, especially at this lofty level of the financial tower.

As we saw whilst putting Mark and Lisa through some horrible scenarios during the insurance and emergency fund chapters, there is so much that can happen between now and retirement: you could suffer ill health; you could have an unplanned addition to the family; you could quit your job; you could actually decide to work for longer because, god forbid, you enjoy it!

This is why the most important step regarding retirement is putting a plan in place.

Then the second, and most important, step is continuously reviewing your plans up to *and* during retirement. This is an absolute necessity to ensure your plan evolves as your life does.

Key points to remember

- When it comes to retirement, be wary of burying your head in the sand.
- Plan for retirement – this couldn't be more important!
- Continuously review said plans throughout retirement.
- Notice how we have been through this entire chapter with barely a mention of the 'P' word. Lots of planning has been covered, but very little on pensions. That is because pensions form only part of your plan.
- This isn't intended to be a science. It is intended to help you with the art of prioritisation and, as a result, planning.

6 Legacy

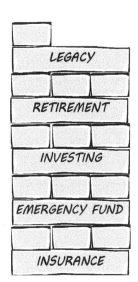

Just as I asked you not to worry when you started the previous chapter on retirement, please do not think this chapter will contain lots of information about trust funds and inheritance tax.

As I keep saying, the purpose of this book is to help you prioritise and build a solid foundation for your financial tower. So, jumping ahead to those heavy topics would be counterintuitive and harmful to your Plan A.

Moreover, investments and retirement planning usually steal the limelight. This chapter is all about an area that is not often considered.

The irony of money

There is a great irony to how we behave with money. Once we have overcome the hurdles of prioritisation to get to this point ...

- protecting our ability to earn an income
- building an emergency fund
- investing for the future
- planning for retirement

... we then begin to think about how we give it all away!

Remember Maslow (the man with a moustache, fetish for pyramids)? In the same way that Maslow stated it is futile to think about creativity and spontaneity when you have not secured food, water and shelter, the same applies to money; you cannot give something away if you haven't got it to give away in the first place.

Nevertheless, it appears that we humans, once we have satisfied all of our other needs, have a final need to satisfy – giving what we have to the people we love, knowing they will benefit from it. Now, this is certainly something we are not taught in school. Instead, we are heavily influenced by the examples set by our family, peers, the cultural norms we are surrounded by and, importantly, our individual financial circumstances.

Bringing it back to Mark and Lisa

Mark and Lisa stated that, when they pass away, they would like their children to inherit their house in equal shares.

Obviously, that will be after the second of them passes away, as that person will still need somewhere to live after the first has gone. The same applies to the savings that they had built up, along with any other assets they own.[6]

When I asked them why they had made this decision, they stated that was what their parents had done for them.

Now, there is nothing incorrect about Mark and Lisa's plans, as there is no right or wrong answer on this topic.

---

6 For clarity, when I refer to "assets" during this chapter, I am referring to your house, savings, investments or anything of value that you could pass on to others in the form of inheritance after your death.

However, I feared that they were simply copying the example left by their parents, like a habit.

So, I highlighted some things they may not have considered when planning how they would like to give away their worldly possessions upon death.

I have broken down the points I made to Mark and Lisa into four areas and will share them with you now.

1) Tenants of your own assets

We Brits seem determined to buy our own home. Culturally, in Britain, it is a symbol of achievement, from which we derive great pride. Then, once we have finally repaid the mortgage, we proudly proclaim, 'it's the kids' inheritance'.

So, I asked Mark and Lisa rhetorically, 'doesn't that make you tenants in your own home?'

Mark and Lisa replied, 'well, we've never thought about it like that. But now you mention it, it does sound pretty ridiculous.'

I will reiterate, there is no right or wrong answer when it comes to giving away your assets. However, I think you should make plans only after becoming aware of the pros and cons. So, just think about that again. You work bloody hard for decades, holding down jobs that you sometimes hate, with people you sometimes despise, just to repay your mortgage.

When you are brave enough, you jump ship to another employer, with a better wage and slightly nicer employees.

When you have kids, one of the parents generally stops working, at least during parental leave, to rear your precious offspring.

If you have more than one child, it can be years, or decades, until both parents return to full-time work, throughout which period both are acutely aware that the mortgage is being paid by the sole 'breadwinner'.

You bob about in the wavy waters of work, weathering recessions, promotions, redundancies and pay rises. You do *so* much to make sure you and your family keep a roof over your heads throughout. Yet, at the end of this arduous journey, you aim to give it away to your children in equal parts once you and your partner pass away. Therefore, you are essentially tenants in your own home, and your children are the landlords. Well, not quite, but you get the point.

This principle applies to *all* your assets, not just your home. But as Brits this example resonates with us most profoundly, as our obsession with the good old 'bricks and mortar' is hardwired into us.

Now, you'll probably be asking, 'OK, so if we don't give away the house when we're dead, what do we pass on instead, and when?' That is a great question! And the reason someone generally says 'great question' is because they don't have the answer.

In this case, there is no exception to the rule. I am *not* going to answer that question, as the spectra of answers could form a book in themselves. Instead, it would be a wise idea to create a plan with a financial adviser who deals with estate planning, to make a plan specifically for you.

Seriously, this isn't a cop-out.

If we come back to the point of this book – prioritising your finances in a way that creates a steroid-strength financial tower, which ensures your Plan A comes to fruition – it wouldn't be useful to throw heaps of estate-planning jargon at you when it is likely at this point that you will be focussing lower down your tower, as the majority of people are.

So, this really is the most helpful thing I can tell you right now:

1. Rethink your British instincts to just give away the house
2. Prioritise making your tower structurally sound
3. Then (and only then) get some help to put an estate plan in place by professionals.

Please note: an estate plan is much more than writing a will, so refrain from DIY. Also, when I use the phrase 'estate planner', you don't have to be Lord and Lady of the Highclere Castle estate (aka Downton Abbey). This will become especially pertinent if you read the next point on this topic ...

2) Beneficiaries not using it wisely

Let's assume that you *do* want to pass on your assets once you've died. You have made the conscious (not habitual) decision to give your assets to someone else, or even an institution, such as a charity. Because the recipients have benefitted from your generosity, they are referred to as your beneficiaries.

Question – how will you be sure your beneficiaries will use the money wisely?

Answer – there *are* ways of ensuring that your beneficiaries receive guidance on your behalf, to make sure they spend the money as you intended. Predominantly, the options available include utilising trusts, so that trustees can be installed to make decisions on how the money is distributed on your behalf when you are no longer alive.

Now, I'll avoid the pitfall of going into too much detail on trusts, because, again, that is a book in itself. Needless to say, if it's your wish for people to be responsible for ensuring your money is spent wisely by your chosen recipients after your death, it's wise to use the help of a financial adviser who you have confidence in to create a plan for your estate.

3) Never getting to see the good that the money does

Now, let's assume that you have made the conscious decision to pass on certain assets to beneficiaries upon your death, and you have put in place ways of ensuring they spend it wisely.

This is a much more deliberate and controlled plan than before. Yet do you see the flaw in this plan? You won't get the satisfaction of seeing the beneficiaries use the money to good effect. Just think of the joy you could experience by helping your children onto the property ladder, supporting grandchildren with their university costs, or enabling a charity to put your assets to good use for the people (or animals) they serve.

You have worked so hard to build up those assets over a long period of time. Surely, when giving them away, you should experience the happiness they bring to others in return for your favour. What do you think? Once again, there is no right or wrong answer.

However, through eperience, I find people, when planning their estates, rarely think about the satisfaction it has the potential to bring them.

Obviously, the caveat to giving away an asset before you die, such as savings or your house, could be the slight niggle of needing it yourself whilst you are alive!

So, the challenge here is to explore whether you could engineer your finances another way in advance.

Again, this brings us perilously close to a topic that could expand quicker than the universe, so I will tread carefully and, again, recommend that, if this is something you'd like to explore, use a financial adviser that you trust to guide you through the options available to you.

4) Unwanted recipients

Finally, when I look at people's estate plans, I rarely find that they have taken into consideration potentially unwanted recipients getting their grubby little mitts on their hard-earned assets.

I asked Mark and Lisa, 'do you think your three daughters will get married?' They immediately answered 'yes', elongating and inflecting this one-syllable word to reassure me that the answer was obvious. I then cautiously asked, 'have you ever considered the possibility of one of them getting divorced?'

They replied in a considered tone, 'well, we haven't thought about it specifically, but a large number of marriages do end in divorce, so we suppose it is a possibility'.

I then proceeded to explain that my question regarding divorce was not intended to cause distress to Mark and Lisa. In fact, it was to point out that distress could be caused if one of their daughters were to divorce their spouse after inheriting assets from their parents.

You see, rarely do parents and grandparents consider that, once they give away their assets to their children and grandchildren, a large amount could end up in the hands of an unwanted recipient, due to the dividing of assets that occurs when a marriage ends.

This could occur either before or after your death. Either way, it would cause a lot of upset to see assets that were earned over a long period of time pass to an unwanted recipient as they part ways from the family.

Inherited assets are some of the hardest earned, but potentially some of the most vulnerable. They are also some of the most overlooked. I am frequently told, 'well, I'll be dead, so it won't be my problem to make sure people get what they think they deserve', when discussing whether assets inherited by their bloodline could end up in the hands of unwanted recipients.

I'll repeat that common response, as you may have even said it yourself, out loud or in your head, 'well, I'll be dead, so it won't be my problem'.

I always find this baffling; if a person wouldn't give money to an individual if they requested it, why would they want the same individual to receive the money after their own death? In fact, in both situations the person who earned the assets has the decision as to who will own them next.

If your beneficiaries don't deplete the assets themselves, passing them on to their children, this could result in the assets being eroded by inheritance tax through the generations, as His Majesty's Revenue and Customs (HMRC), the department of UK Government responsible for collecting taxes, take a share. Do you want HMRC to take a slice?

Another example is bankruptcy. Inherited assets could be used to repay debts amassed by the beneficiary. Is this how you would want them to be spent?

Finally, your assets might not make it that far in the first place. If you need to go into domiciliary care, your assets will be assessed. The government will essentially determine if you have enough, in the form of a house or savings, for example, to fund your care before their support will kick in. Is that why you saved hard and worked all those years to repay your mortgage?

Again, there are ways of preventing this from happening. The first step is to stop saying 'doesn't matter, I'll be dead', the second is to make a plan using the help of a financial adviser.

Key points to remember

- When it comes to passing our assets on when we die, we rarely think about different options. We just tend to follow family members or societal norms.

- We rarely think about watching someone enjoy their inheritance from us whilst we're still alive and kicking, which *is* an option.

- When it comes to deciding whether or not to pass on your house, speak to a financial adviser first. And remember, a castle or manor house is certainly not needed to qualify for an estate planning meeting.

- If you do decide to pass everything on once you've died, there are ways of ensuring that your beneficiaries receive guidance on your behalf, to make sure they spend the money as you intended.

- To stop your assets falling into the wrong hands, being gobbled up by HMRC or being used as your 'care allowance', speak to a financial adviser and put a plan in place.

7 Feeling better about your money?

So, there you have it – the Assembly Guide for your money.

Now, I can't stand it when a closing chapter is a book within itself. You've got this far, so I think you should be rewarded with a concise recap of the key lessons from this book.

Concise recap time

- We have walked through what we are not taught at school about finance, learning how to correctly prioritise your money to achieve your ideal future – your Plan A.

- Maslow stated that society pressures us to leapfrog up the tower of needs more quickly than is necessary, which jeopardises its structural integrity and, as a result, your Plan A.

- In Maslow's time, the societal pressures he faced would have forced him to question, 'shall I buy a television?' 'Can I afford to buy a new car?' 'Is a house phone a good idea?' In contrast, nowadays society expects us to have the biggest TV, the newest car, the latest phone. Although these pressures are completely different from those faced by Maslow in 1943 ... Wait, are they? No, they are almost identical!

- Due to continuous pressures via social media, advertising, emails and websites, it is crucial to be aware that you will inevitably be exposed to many different people and things that want more of your money.

- You have witnessed that Mark and Lisa were also exposed to these pressures. However, when asked to reflect upon each of them, they stated that the pressures were not moving them in the direction of achieving their Plan A. In fact, almost all were putting their Plan A at risk.

- We've determined that your health is your biggest asset, not your home, as health enables you to earn an income, which is worth more than the value of your home (and pays for it!).

- Almost every thought you have about the future is based on the assumption that you will be healthy enough to earn an income to fund your way there. Your tower needs a solid foundation to stand upon. Your ability to earn an income supports the rest of the tower. So, insure your health to ensure you always receive your income.

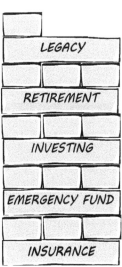

- Next, ask yourself the following questions regularly:
  a) What are the most important things to you in life?
  b) What does money mean to you?

- The answers set your compass and provide your North Star. When you are tempted by the pressures that society puts upon you, just ask yourself these questions and you will realise that the inanimate item you are considering purchasing (usually from Amazon) is nowhere near as important as retiring before the ever-increasing state pension age.

- Thereafter, the principles that I have shared with you start to become self-explanatory. You are solidifying each rung of the tower before moving on to the next.

I will leave you with three things I like to consistently remind my clients, including Mark and Lisa:

1. Life continuously changes, meaning there is no such thing as a perfect plan – so review it continuously to ensure it remains up to date.
2. Not every decision is financial, so keep in mind your North Star to guide you toward your Plan A.
3. Remember to enjoy yourself in the meantime, because the worst time to spend your money is when you're too old to enjoy it – you can't take it with you.

Do you feel better about your money now?

Feel free to contact me...

Remember, if there has been something in this book that has made you want a hand getting that 'tidy house / tidy mind' feeling about your finances, please feel free to contact me and I will be happy to help.

By scanning this QR code you can:

- send me an email
- come along to my next event
- join my informative monthly newsletter, *The Reality Cheque*
- connect with me on LinkedIn
- follow me on Facebook.

The End

References

Buffet, Warren (2005), Berkshire Hathaway Letter to Shareholders. Available at: berkshirehathaway.com/letters/2005ltr.pdf

Maslow, Abraham (1943), 'A Theory of Human Motivation'. Available at: psychclassics.yorku.ca/Maslow/motivation.htm

Morgan Stanley Capital Intermational -MSCI (2019), 'World: The Modern Index Strategy'. Available at: msci.com/documents/1296102/15179875/MSCI-MIS-World-Apr2019-cbr-en.pdf/b6fc1c6d-2c77-da73-21b9-4e639697b0dc?t=1560150686746

Office of National Statistics (2022), Life Expectancy Calculator. Available at: ons.gov.uk/peoplepopulationandcommunity/healthandsocialcare/healthandlifeexpectancies/articles/lifeexpectancycalculator/2019-06-07

Notes

9 781739 427702